ALL ABOUT WILD ANIMALS

Kingfisher Books, Grisewood & Dempsey Ltd,
Elsley House, 24–30 Great Titchfield Street,
London W1P 7AD

First published in paperback in 1993 by Kingfisher Books
10 9 8 7 6 5 4 3 2 1
Originally published in hardback in 1991 by Kingfisher Books

Text copyright © Grisewood & Dempsey Ltd 1991
Illustrations copyright © Peter Barrett 1991

All rights reserved. No part of this publication
may be reproduced, stored in a retrieval system or
transmitted by any means, electronic, mechanical,
photocopying or otherwise, without the prior
permission of the publisher.

BRITISH CATALOGUING IN PUBLICATION DATA
A catalogue record for this book is
available from the British Library

ISBN 1 85697 003 5

Edited by Camilla Hallinan
Designed by Ben White
Phototypeset by Wyvern Typesetting Ltd, Bristol
Colour separations by Scantrans Pte Ltd, Singapore
Printed in Spain

MICHAEL CHINERY

ALL ABOUT WILD ANIMALS

Illustrated by
Peter Barrett

Kingfisher Books

Contents

What is a wild animal? 8

Where animals live 10

In a tree 12

In the sea 14

Animals move 16

Animals that fly 18

Animals feed 20

Animal defences 22

Octopus defends itself 24

Animals have babies 26   Large families 28   Elephant grows up 30

Animals together 32   Hunters 34   Smell and hearing 36

Sight and other senses 38   Clever animals 40
Animals learn 42   Finding out more 44
Index 45

What is a wild animal?

You might think that a wild animal should be as big as a giraffe or as fierce as a crocodile.

But a butterfly is a wild animal.

And so is a harvest mouse.

Wild animals do not have to be big or fierce.

Hummingbird

Crocodile

Butterfly

Beetle

Flamingo

Harvest mouse

Skunk

In fact, a wild animal is simply one that is not looked after by people on a farm or kept as a pet.

One of the most amazing things about animals is their variety of shape and size and colour.

Just look at all the fish below, and then compare them with the other animals on these pages.

Where animals live

Animals live almost everywhere – in the water as well as on the land. Each kind of animal has its preferred habitat. This is the place where it finds its food and spends most of its life.

Bald eagles live high in the mountains of North America. They nest in trees or on cliffs.

Koalas live only in certain types of eucalyptus, or gum trees, in Australia.

Earthworms have long, slender bodies. They spend their lives tunnelling through the soil.

Polar bears live in the frozen Arctic. Their thick coats keep them warm.

Some spiders live in our houses. They often fall into the bath when they are looking for water.

Paramecium live in water but they are so small that they can be seen only through a microscope.

Sand lizards spend their time in the hot sunshine of deserts and other dry places.

In a tree

Owl

Woodpecker

Wood warbler

Butterfly

Jay

Trees provide food and homes for many kinds of animals.

Hundreds of different kinds of insects may live in one oak tree. They feed on every part of the tree, especially the leaves and the fruits and seeds. Some tunnel through the solid wood of the trunk.

Squirrel

Spiders and birds eat many of the insects. Even the insects tunnelling in the trunk are not safe from the woodpeckers.

Woodpeckers and owls nest in holes in the tree trunk. Other birds and squirrels build nests in the branches. A badger may make its home under the roots.

Shrew

Hedgehog

Worms, slugs and many other small animals feed on the fallen leaves. Hedgehogs and shrews then eat the slugs and worms, and owls and foxes eat the shrews. So you can see that trees are very important for wild animals.

Badger

In the sea

More animals live in the sea than anywhere else.

The best place to see some of these sea creatures is on a rocky seashore, although this is not an easy place for animals to live. They are battered by the waves, and they must be able to survive out of water when the tides go out.

Limpets cling tightly to the rocks. They are able to hold a little water under their shells when they are uncovered by the tides.

In the sea most animals live near the surface, where the water contains millions of minute floating plants and animals called plankton. Other small animals feed on the plankton. Then they are eaten by larger animals, such as jellyfish, herrings and shrimps.

Fish that live on the seabed, such as plaice, are often flat and the same colour as their background.

In the deepest parts of the ocean it is very dark and there are no plants. The fish and other animals that live there are mostly a dark colour, and many have weird shapes. Some even have lights like little torches to help them to find food and mates.

Limpet

Jellyfish

Plankton

Herring

Shrimp

Plaice

15

Animals move

In the water, most animals swim by using their fins and flippers. The squid can also push itself along by squirting out water.

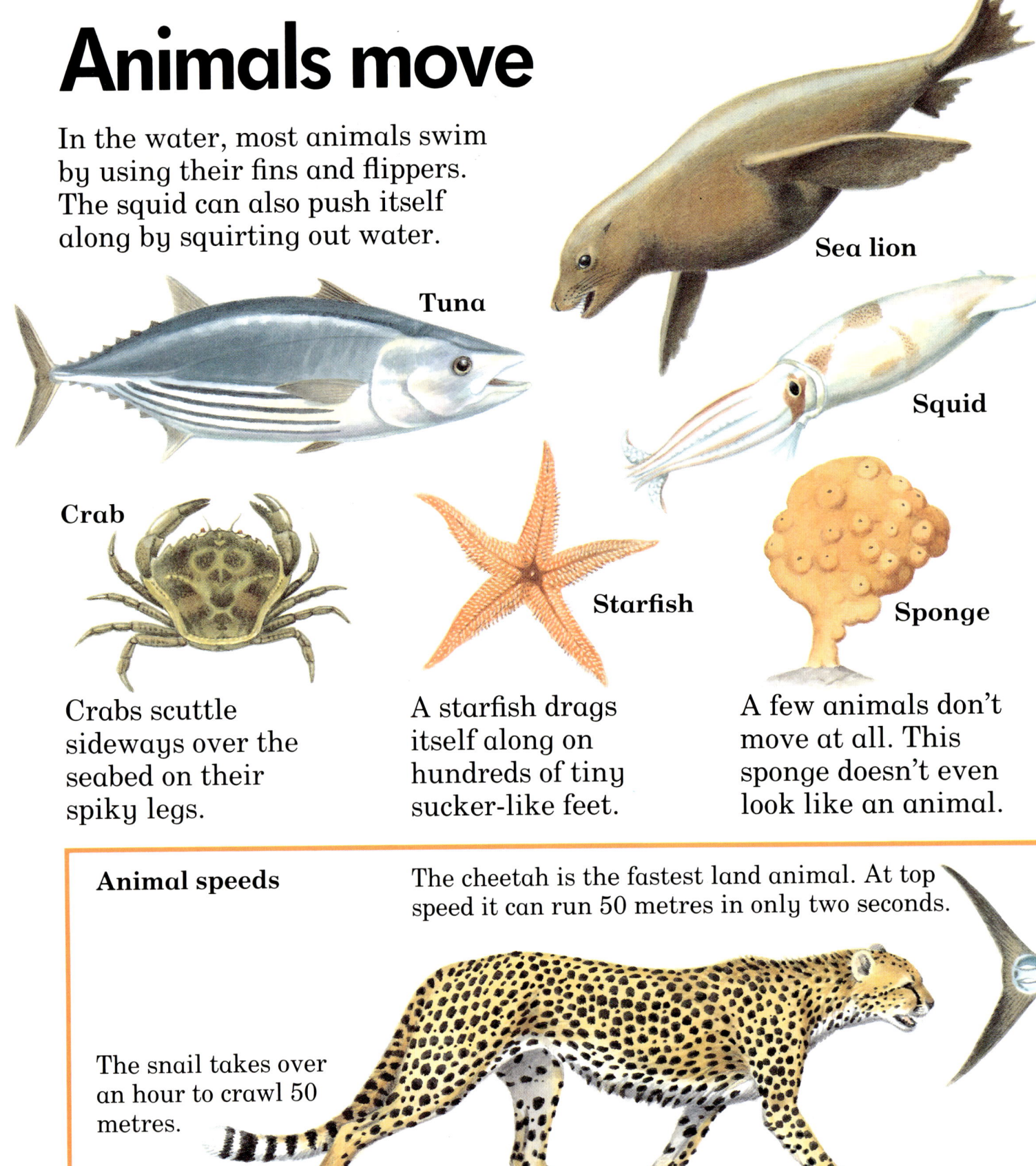

Sea lion

Tuna

Squid

Crab

Starfish

Sponge

Crabs scuttle sideways over the seabed on their spiky legs.

A starfish drags itself along on hundreds of tiny sucker-like feet.

A few animals don't move at all. This sponge doesn't even look like an animal.

Animal speeds

The cheetah is the fastest land animal. At top speed it can run 50 metres in only two seconds.

The snail takes over an hour to crawl 50 metres.

On land most animals move about on two or more legs. Ostriches walk on two legs and frogs on four. Insects, such as crickets, have six legs, spiders have eight and centipedes have lots of legs. Snakes have no legs at all.

Climbing animals use their arms and even their tails to move through the trees.

The sailfish is the fastest fish in the world. It can swim at over 100 kilometres an hour.

The peregrine falcon can swoop after its prey at well over 150 kilometres an hour.

Animals that fly

Insects, bats and birds are the only animals that fly. Most insects, such as dragonflies and moths, have four wings. But flies, such as hover-flies, have only two.

Hover-fly

Ladybird

Ladybirds keep their wings folded under their brightly coloured wing-cases, until they need to fly.

Dragonfly

Bats are very agile fliers. They chase moths at night and catch them in mid-air. Their wings are made of skin stretched over very long fingers.

Bat

Moth

The shape of a bird's wing can tell you something about the way the bird flies.

Birds, such as wrens, that dart about in trees and bushes have short and rather pointed wings.

Wren

Long-distance fliers, such as the albatross, must save their energy by gliding as much as they can.

Long, narrow wings are best for this kind of flight.

Albatross

Buzzard

Buzzards circle high in the sky as they look for prey. They have broad wings with long feathers at the tips.

Not all birds can fly. Cassowaries cannot fly, but they run very fast.

The penguin cannot fly, but uses its wings to swim under the water.

Animals feed

Animals need energy to grow and to stay alive. They get energy from their food. Many animals eat only plants. They are called herbivores. Some, such as pandas and gorillas, eat leaves and stems, but others, such as parrots, prefer fruits and seeds.

Panda

Gorilla

Parrot

Meat-eaters are called carnivores. The lion hunts zebra for its food.

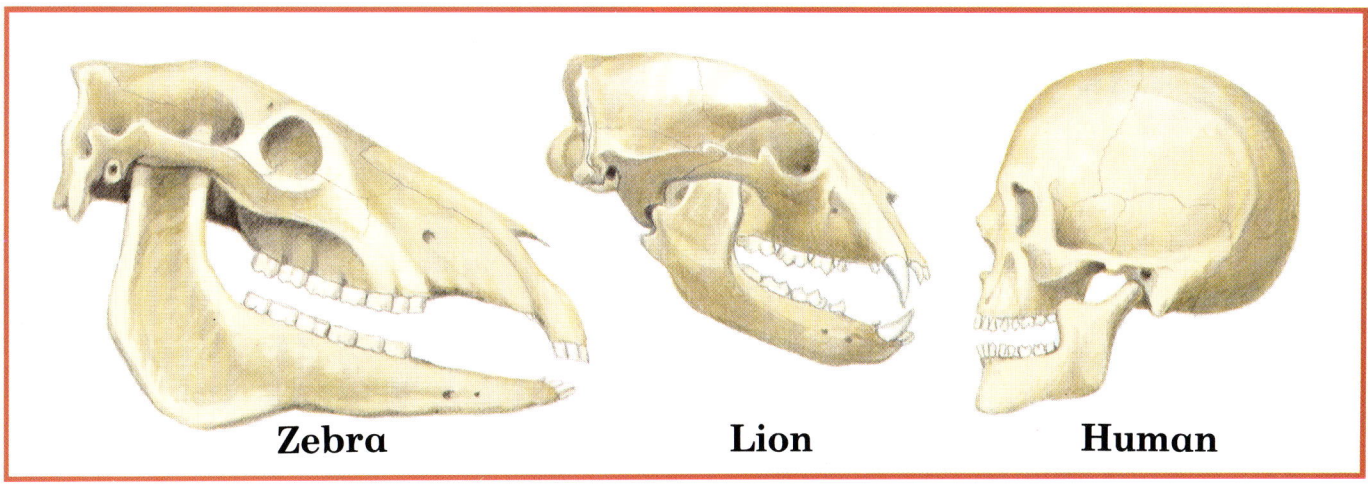

Zebra **Lion** **Human**

You can tell what sort of food some animals eat by looking at their teeth. Zebras and other herbivores have big, flat teeth for grinding up grass. Lions and other carnivores have stabbing teeth for killing their prey and sharp back teeth for slicing the flesh. Omnivores eat plants and animals. They have both cutting teeth and grinding teeth. Our own teeth are like this.

Animal defences

All animals need to defend themselves against the hungry carnivores that are always hunting for food.

Some animals have clever ways of protecting themselves from their enemies.

Musk oxen protect their young from wolves by forming a circle around them. Their horns all point outwards, so the wolves will be in danger if they attack them.

When the peacock butterfly is resting on a branch with its wings closed it is not very easy to see.

But when the butterfly is alarmed it opens its wings, flashing big eye-spots which frighten its enemies.

The wasp defends itself by stinging its attackers.

The porcupine turns its back on its enemies and points its sharp quills at them.

The armadillo has bony plates on its back like a coat of armour.

Many animals simply run away at great speed to escape from their enemies.

This gazelle confuses the cheetah by leaping in the air and changing direction.

Octopus defends itself

An octopus would make a delicious meal for a hungry fish. But it has several ways of defending itself.

The octopus lives in a hole on the seabed. It leaves its hiding place only to catch food, such as a crab or shrimp that passes by.

As soon as the octopus has left its hole to creep over the seabed, it can be seen by any passing fish.

So it quickly changes colour to match its background. It becomes nearly invisible.

But too late: a moray eel has seen the movement and swims over to investigate. The octopus changes again, suddenly becoming very pale and spreading its arms so that it looks enormous. The eel is startled and it turns away.

The grouper fish does not give up so easily. But the octopus still has another trick with which to defend itself.

It squirts a cloud of black ink into the water. This confuses the grouper, so the octopus can swim away to find another safe hole to hide in.

Animals have babies

Every baby animal starts life as an egg in its mother's body. Some eggs grow inside the mother, and then she gives birth to her babies. But most animals lay their eggs and the babies break out of the eggs when they are ready.

The condor chick hatches from its egg after about eight weeks. It looks a bit like its parent, although it doesn't have proper feathers yet.

Some babies don't look like their parents at all. The caterpillar hatching from its egg is a baby butterfly. One day it will turn into a colourful butterfly like the one on the flower.

Mammal babies usually grow inside their mothers for quite a long time. The baby rhinoceros grows in its mother's body for about eighteen months before it is born.

Marsupial mammals are very small when they are born. A new-born kangaroo is only 2.5 centimetres long. It crawls into its mother's pouch and feeds on her milk for about eight months.

Large families

Some animals have only one baby at a time, but most animals have several.

The rabbit may have as many as eight babies. Feeding and looking after all of them is hard work.

Many animals never see their babies. Sea turtles come ashore to lay their eggs in the sand.

They lay lots of eggs and leave them to hatch on their own. The babies then have to cross the sand and find the sea all by themselves. Many are eaten by birds on the way, and only a few reach the water. This is why the turtles have to lay lots of eggs.

The frog lays hundreds of eggs and then swims away. Many of the eggs are eaten by other animals.

Tadpoles hatch from the eggs. Most of them get eaten, but a few of them survive and turn into little frogs.

The salmon lays thousands of eggs. The babies that hatch each have a yolk sac which provides them with food for about six weeks.

Elephant grows up

An elephant baby takes 22 months – that's almost two years – to grow inside its mother's body. The new-born calf is only about a metre high and it can walk when it is just an hour old. The calf grows quickly on its mother's rich milk.

The baby lives with its mother and other elephants in a herd.

Elephants love water. The calves squirt it at each other with their trunks. But if they squirt the adults they get a smack to teach them how to behave. Their trunks are short at first, but they soon grow and the animals learn how to use them to collect leafy branches from the trees.

Animals together

Some animals live in family groups for all or most of their lives. Some live in even bigger groups. There are many good reasons for living in groups like this.

For example, a large group of animals has many eyes, ears and noses to tell them when predators appear. These Canada geese have spotted an Arctic fox and are calling loudly to warn the other geese. The whole flock will soon take off to escape.

Hunting in groups often means there is a better chance of getting food. A pack of wolves can easily catch and kill a large caribou.

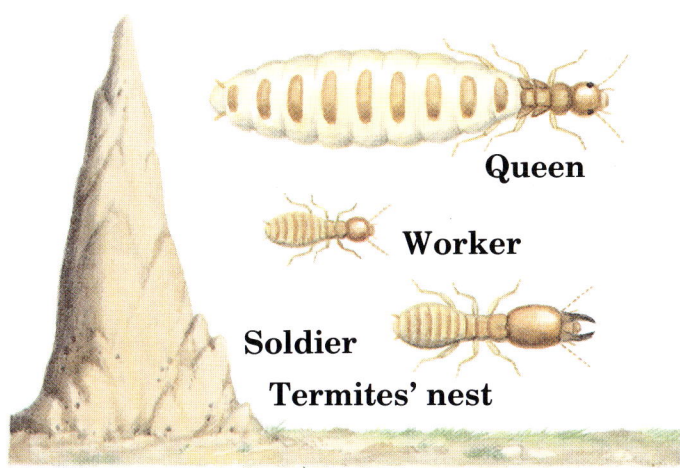

Termites are insects that live and work together in huge family groups. The workers build big nests and the big-jawed soldiers defend them. The queen is the mother of all the workers and soldiers.

But not all animals that live together help each other. Razorbills nest close together only because there is not much room on the cliffs where they live.

Here are some names for groups of animals. Can you think of other ones?

A pride of lions

A shoal of sardines

A herd of bison

A troop of baboons

Hunters

Killer whales hunt in groups called pods. There may be as many as 40 whales in a pod.

These whales are chasing a school of salmon. They signal to each other with sounds and gradually herd the salmon into shallow water near the shore. The whales dart into the trapped school of salmon and eat as many as they can, before swimming back out to sea.

The tiger hunts alone. It feeds mainly on deer and wild pigs. Its stripes help it to hide in the waving grasses as it stalks its prey. When it is close enough, the tiger springs forward with tremendous power and seizes its prey.

Smell and hearing

To find food, avoid enemies, and have babies, animals need to know what is happening around them. They find out by using one or more of their senses. The sense of smell is one of the most important senses. Some animals can find their way around almost entirely by smell.

The squirrel can smell if a nut is good or bad. It doesn't waste time opening bad ones.

Snakes pick up the smell of their prey by flicking out their tongues.

This brown bear has picked up the scent of a female. He will track her down with his nose.

The salmon returning from the sea uses smell to find the river where it was born.

Hearing is another very important sense.

Sounds travel faster and farther in water than in air. Dolphins can hear each other calling many kilometres away, so a mother can always find her own baby.

Birds' songs bring males and females together at nesting time.

Night animals hunt by listening for sounds. This owl flies very quietly and its ears can pick up the slightest rustle of a mouse in the grass. It also has excellent eyesight.

Sight and other senses

Animals use their eyes to find food and to watch for danger. Not all animals can see in colour, but they can recognize shapes and some are very good at spotting movements from a long way away.

The kestrel hovering high in the air can spot a vole, or even a beetle, on the ground below.

Two forward-looking eyes help the lynx to judge distances and to leap accurately on to its prey.

Flies are hard to catch because their big eyes can see all around them. Their bristles also feel the air move when something approaches.

Bees are attracted to flowers by their colours, but they don't always see the colour we do. This yellow flower looks blue to a bee.

The lobster finds its way around using the long, sensitive feelers, or antennae, on its head.

The panther has whiskers which are sensitive to the slightest touch.

The slender stripe on each side of this cod picks up vibrations in the water and so tells the fish about the other things around it.

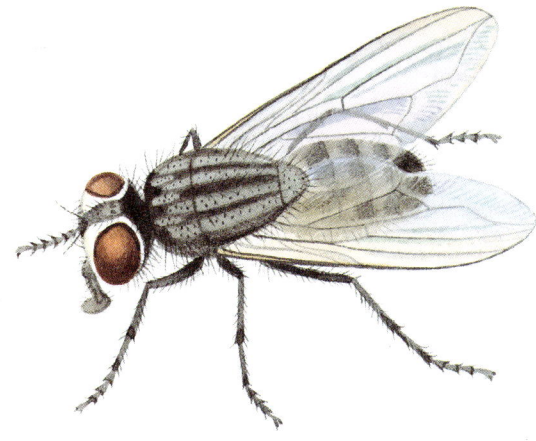

A house-fly actually tastes food with its feet. When the fly lands on something, special nerves in its feet test the surface and tell the fly whether it is good to eat or not. If it is good to eat, the fly sticks out its tongue and starts to feed.

Clever animals

The brain is like a computer. It has lots of programs for hunting, hiding, sleeping and finding a mate.

A tiny flea needs a brain to control its actions just as much as a big hippopotamus does.

Flea
(15 times life size)

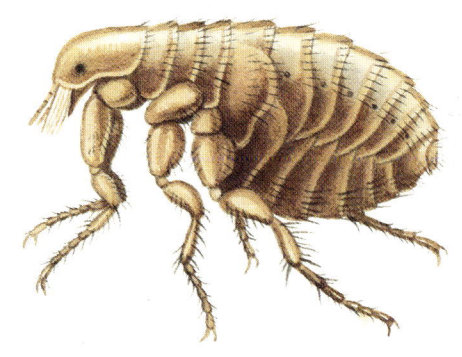

Some animals are born with all the programs they need. The spider, for example, knows exactly how to make its web as soon as it is born. This is called instinct.

But many animals add to their set of programs as they grow up. They do this by learning new things – often from their parents.

The most important thing the brain does is to choose the right program for a particular situation. The brain of a feeding deer will tell it to run away when it sees or hears a puma approach, even if the deer is still hungry.

Animals learn

This young chimp is watching its mother catch termites by poking a stick into the termites' nest. The young chimp will soon learn to do this for itself, and will be able to collect its own meal of juicy termites.

The blue tit catchs a poisonous caterpillar. It will spit it out and always remember that yellow and black caterpillars taste nasty.

Fox cubs love to chase and jump on each other in fun. This is a good way to learn how to catch their prey when they grow up.

When bees leave the hive to collect nectar and pollen, they circle around for a while and learn the trees and other landmarks that will guide them safely home again.

Finding out more

Zoologists are scientists who study animals. This zoologist learns more about fish by swimming with them in the water.

You can find out more about animals by visiting a wildlife park, a zoo or an aquarium.

You can read books about animals and go out into the countryside to look for them yourselves.

And on television you can watch many of the wonderful nature programmes about the fascinating world of animals.

Index

A
albatross 19
angelfish 9
Arctic fox 32
armadillo 23

B
baboon 33
badger 13
bald eagle 10
bat 18
bear 11, 36
bee 38, 43
beetle 8
bird 13, 19, 37
bison 33
blue tit 43
boa 17
brown bear 36
butterfly 8, 13, 22, 26
buzzard 19

C
Canada geese 32
caribou 32
carnivore 21, 22
cassowary 19
caterpillar 26, 43
centipede 17
cheetah 16, 23
chimpanzee 43
clownfish 9
cod 39
condor 26
crab 16
cricket 17
crocodile 8

D
deer 12, 35, 41
dog 9
dolphin 37
dragonfly 18

E
eagle 10
earthworm 10
eel 24
egg 26, 28, 29
elephant 30, 31

F
falcon 17
fish 9, 14, 15, 24, 25
flamingo 8
flea 40
fly 18, 38, 39
fox 12, 32, 43
frog 17, 29

G
gazelle 23
geese 32
gibbon 17
giraffe 9
gorilla 20
grouper 25

H
habitat 10, 11
harvest mouse 8
hedgehog 13
herbivore 20, 21
herring 15
hippopotamus 40
hover-fly 19
hummingbird 8

I
insect 13, 17, 18, 33

J
jay 13
jellyfish 15

K
kangaroo 27
kestrel 38
killer whale 34
kitten 9
koala 10

L
ladybird 18
limpet 15
lion 21, 33
lizard 11
lobster 39
lynx 38

M
mammal 27
marsupial 27
monkey 17
moray eel 24
moth 18
mouse 8
musk ox 22

O
octopus 24, 25
omnivore 21
ostrich 17
owl 13, 37
ox 22

P
panda 20
panther 39
paramecium 11
parrot 20
parrot fish 9
peacock butterfly 22
penguin 19
peregrine falcon 17
plaice 15
pig 9
pipefish 9
plankton 15
polar bear 11
porcupine 23
puma 41

R
rabbit 28
razorbill 33
rhinoceros 27

S
sailfish 17
salamander 9
salmon 29, 34, 36
sand lizard 11
sardine 33
seahorse 9
sea lion 16
sea turtle 28
shrew 13
shrimp 15
skunk 8
snail 16
snake 17, 36
spider 11, 17, 41
spider monkey 17
sponge 16
squid 16
squirrel 13, 36
starfish 16

T
tadpole 29
termite 33, 42
tiger 35
tuna 16
turtle 28

W
warbler 13
wasp 23
whale 34
wolf 32
woodpecker 13
wood warbler 13
worm 10
wren 19

Z
zebra 21
zoologist 44

45

MORE KINGFISHER PAPERBACKS FOR YOU TO ENJOY

Also in the All About Series:

ALL ABOUT BABY ANIMALS
ISBN 0 86272 525 9   £3.50

ALL ABOUT FARM ANIMALS
ISBN 0 86272 520 8   £3.50

ALL ABOUT DINOSAURS
ISBN 0 86272 649 2   £3.50

ALL ABOUT THINGS PEOPLE DO
ISBN 0 86272 524 0   £3.50

ALL ABOUT ME
ISBN 0 86272 775 8   £3.50

ALL ABOUT OUR WORLD
ISBN 0 86272 776 6   £3.50

And in the Magic Bus Series:

THE MAGIC BUS AT THE WATERWORKS
ISBN 086272 791 X   £2.95

THE MAGIC BUS INSIDE THE HUMAN BODY
ISBN 086272 788 X   £2.99

THE MAGIC BUS LOST IN THE SOLAR SYSTEM
ISBN 086272 867 3   £2.99

THE MAGIC BUS INSIDE THE EARTH
ISBN 086272 866 5   £2.99

Kingfisher Books are available from most bookshops or by post from:

KINGFISHER CASH SALES
P.O. BOX 11
FALMOUTH
CORNWALL TR10 9EN

If you wish, you may fax your order to FAX NO: 0326 376423. Please state your name and address and list the titles required.

Payments can be made as follows: Cheque, postal order (payable to Kingfisher Books) or by credit card Visa/Access (Mastercard), stating card number and expiry date, PLEASE DO NOT SEND CASH OR CURRENCY.

Please include with your payment the following amount for postage and packing:

UK customers (including BFPO):
one book.. £1.00
second book ....plus £0.50
plus 30p each additional book
 to a maximum charge of £3.00
(7 books plus)

Overseas (including Eire):
one book... £2.00
second book ....plus £1.00
plus 50p each additional book

While every effort is made to keep prices low, prices of books and postage/packing are subject to change without notice. Kingfisher Books reserves the right to show new retail prices on covers that may differ from those previously advertised here or elsewhere.